W9-ALJ-087

WITHDRAWN

Donated to
SAINT PAUL PUBLIC LIBRARY

YOU'D *never* BELIEVE IT BUT...

a rainbow is a circle

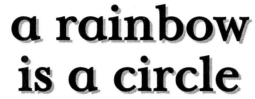

and other facts about color

© Aladdin Books Ltd 1999

Designed and produced by
Aladdin Books Ltd
28 Percy Street
London W1P 0LD

First published in the United States in 1999 by
Copper Beech Books,
an imprint of
The Millbrook Press
2 Old New Milford Road
Brookfield, Connecticut 06804

Designed by
David West Children's Books
Designer
Flick Killerby
Computer Illustrations
Stephen Sweet (Simon Girling & Associates)
Project Editor
Sally Hewitt
Editor
Liz White
Picture Research
Carlotta Cooper
and Brooks Krikler Research

Printed in Belgium
All rights reserved

Library of Congress Cataloging-in-Publication Data
Taylor, Helen (Helen Suzanne), 1963-
a rainbow is a circle : and other facts about color / by Helen
Taylor.
p. cm. — (You'd never believe it but —)
Includes index.
Summary: Introduces colors, exploring primary and
secondary colors, recognizing colors, colors in light, and
more. Includes simple projects.
ISBN 0-7613-3250-2 (lib. bdg.)
1. Color—Juvenile literature. [1. Color.] I. Title. II. Series.
QC495.5 T43   1999   98-49736
535.6—dc21   CIP AC
5 4 3 2 1

YOU'D *never* BELIEVE IT BUT...

a rainbow is a circle

and other facts about color

Helen Taylor

COPPER BEECH BOOKS
BROOKFIELD, CONNECTICUT

Contents

Introduction

Every day you see colors all around you, from dazzling plants and animals to colorful paints or lights. But have you ever thought about how to mix or split colors, or about the different messages colors can give you?

Join Jack and Jo as they learn about primary and secondary colors, rainbow colors, and much, much more.

FUN PROJECTS
Wherever you see this sign, it means that there is a project that you can do.

Each project will help you to understand more about the subject. You'd never believe it but... each project is fun to do, as well.

Color everywhere

The world is a colorful place, with blue skies, green leaves, and brightly colored flowers, birds, and insects. Clothes, toys, cars, and the things you use are often colorful, too. Look all around you. How many different colors can you see? What is your favorite color? Are there any colors you don't like?

My favorite color is yellow.

The world would look very different without color (above). Would it be duller or more interesting? Would it be difficult to live without color?

You'd never believe it but...

There are perhaps as many as ten million different colors; many surround you every day (left).

Guess what my favorite color is.

SHADES OF COLOR

Collect all kinds of colorful objects, including paper and cardboard. Sort them into groups of different colors. Are all the yellow objects exactly the same yellow? What about the blue objects? Every color has many different shades. Make a collage using only yellow objects. Look at how many different shades of yellow there are!

Primary and secondary colors

Red, yellow, and blue are very important colors. They are called the primary colors. You can make lots of other colors by mixing these colors.

red + yellow = orange

yellow + blue = green

red + blue = purple

I want to make orange.

When primary colors are mixed in pairs, the colors they make are called secondary colors. Orange, green, and purple are secondary colors.

You'd never believe it but...

Paints were used many thousands of years ago. Colors called pigments can be found in earth or rocks. Cave painters used these to paint the walls of caves.

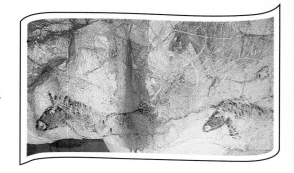

Try mixing red and yellow.

MIXING PAINTS

It is surprising how many colors and shades you can make by mixing different amounts of primary colors together. Try to paint a picture using as many colors as you can make from just the primaries.

Mixing colors

You may not realize it, but often your brain will mix colors together for you! If you make a picture from lots of little different colored dots, your brain mixes the dots together to form new colors. What color do you think your brain will see if you mix red and blue dots?

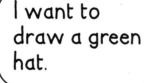
COLOR WHEEL
Try making a color wheel. Start with the primary colors. Then mix each pair of primary colors together to make the secondary color in between. Opposite colors like blue and orange, can look brighter when placed next to each other.

I want to draw a green hat.

You'd never believe it but...

Look at a printed book and you see solid colors, but under a magnifying glass you will see thousands of colored dots.

Use yellow and blue dots.

The French artist Seurat used dots of color to create images in his paintings. If you look at them close up, you only see the dots. But from a distance, the solid color images appear.

Splitting colors

The colored inks used in felt-tip pens are often a mixture of different colors. Usually they are made up of different amounts of primary colors. You can find out which colors were used in each pen.

There's some blue in the green pen.

FINDING COLORS

You will need paper towels, felt-tip pens, and a glass of water. Draw a small dot with each pen on a paper towel. Leave plenty of space between each dot. Drop a small amount of water onto the colored dots. The water spreads out and carries the different colors different distances. How many different colors around each dot can you spot?

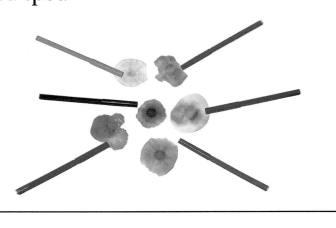

You'd never believe it but...

If ink is left at the scene of a crime, detectives can tell which pen it has come from by splitting the colors in the ink.

Making colors

Dyes have a strong color and are used to color many things. The first dyes were made naturally by boiling plants like onions, grass, and beets. Today we can buy dye in small packets of powdered chemicals. Dyes color paint and the ink in felt-tip pens. Your clothes are colored with dyes too.

Did my sweater come from a yellow sheep?

Some rocks look colorful because they contain colors called pigments. Paints and dyes contain pigments, too, that can be used to change the color of things.

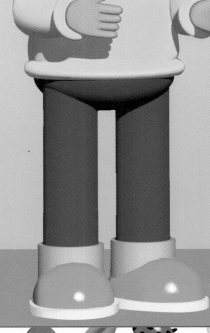

You'd never believe it but...

You can eat small beetles! A bright red dye called cochineal is made from grinding up small beetles. The cochineal beetle is tiny (left) and is used to make some food coloring, so you may have tasted it before!

No! The wool has been dyed yellow.

TIE-DYE A HANDKERCHIEF

Ask an adult to chop up a beet and boil it so that the water turns purple. Tie a string tightly around a handkerchief as shown. Dip it into the water and leave for a few minutes. Take it out and cut the string when it is cool. Dry the handkerchief. Can you see how and where the dye has colored the material a beet color?

Rainbow colors

Mixing colored light produces new colors, too, but in a different way than mixing paints. We often say light is white, but actually, light is made up of all the seven colors of the rainbow: red, orange, yellow, green, blue, indigo, and violet. We call these colors the spectrum.

When the sun shines through raindrops, the water bends the white light and splits it into the different colors. A rainbow appears as a spectrum in the sky.

The sun shining through the water makes a rainbow!

You'd never believe it but...

A rainbow is really a circle, not an arc. You can only see part of the rainbow from the ground. From an airplane a rainbow looks like a circle.

I can see seven different colors.

MAKING RAINBOWS
Blow bubbles in the sunshine. The light makes rainbows on the surfaces of the bubbles.

Recognizing colors

When light shines on an object, some of the rainbow colors are taken in, or absorbed, by it, but other colors bounce back, or reflect, off it. We see the colors that bounce back off an object. This means you can only see colors if light shines on an object.

I can't see the color of my sweater in the dark!

Although we speak of seeing colors of objects, we do not actually see them. We see the light that bounces off them. For example, a red sock looks red because it reflects red light and absorbs the other colors. You only see the red light that reflects off the sock, so it looks red.

You'd never believe it but...

Animals, like cats, that hunt at night cannot see color very well, but their eyes are very good at letting in light, which helps them to find their way in the dark.

> You can see it's yellow if I shine my flashlight on it.

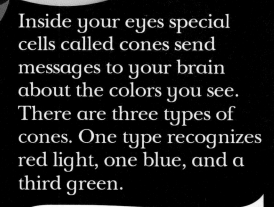

Inside your eyes special cells called cones send messages to your brain about the colors you see. There are three types of cones. One type recognizes red light, one blue, and a third green.

Black and white

Some objects take in, or absorb, all the colors of the rainbow when light shines on them. When this happens, the object looks black. When all the colors of the rainbow bounce back, or reflect, off an object, it looks white.

SPINNING TOP

Cut a circle out of cardboard. Divide it into seven equal sections, and color each section a different rainbow color. Push a short pencil through a hole in the center. Spin the top. What happens? You see white because your brain mixes all the colors of the spectrum together.

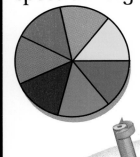

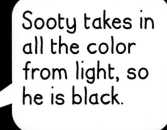

Sooty takes in all the color from light, so he is black.

Light-colored objects reflect a lot of light, but dark colors reflect little or no light. A photographic negative shows these areas in reverse, so black or dark objects look white and white or light objects look black.

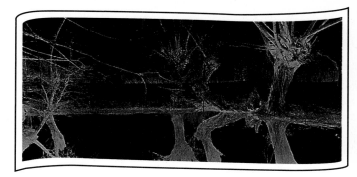

You'd never believe it but...

Over 300 years ago, Sir Isaac Newton proved white light is made from the colors of the rainbow. He split light through a glass prism and showed a spectrum.

Snowy reflects all the colors, that's why he's white.

Colored light

Glass, water, and cellophane are all transparent materials. This means you can see through them. You can still see through transparent materials even if they are colored, but the color makes everything look different.

CHANGING COLOR

Collect some colored cellophane candy wrappers. Flatten them out and look through them one at a time. The colored cellophane becomes a filter. It only lets light of its own color pass through it. If you look at an orange ball through a green filter, the ball looks dark. The green filter only lets green light through; the other colors are blocked so they look dark.

Ooh! Everything looks spooky!

You'd never believe it but...

Colored filters can be put over a camera lens. Areas where there is a lot of light will show up the color of the filter; other areas will appear darker.

Don't worry – it's only green and red lights!

Colored filters are put over spotlights at the theater to make exciting effects on the stage.

Color in plants

Plants help to make the world look bright and colorful. But the colors in plants are not just there to look pretty, they have an important job to do. The stems and leaves of plants contain chlorophyll. It is a pigment that gives plants their green color. Plants use chlorophyll and sunlight to make their own food.

Brightly colored flowers send a message to birds and insects that there is food here! The birds and insects carry pollen from flower to flower. This enables the flowers to make new seeds.

Watch out – a bee!

PLANT CHART
Make a chart of the colors in your yard or nearby park. How many different colored plants are there? Which seem more popular with the birds, bees, and butterflies? Why do you think this is?

color	bird	bee	butterfly
	✓	✓✓	
		✓	
			✓✓
	✓		

You'd never believe it but...

Flowers of the yellow bee orchid are colored to look like a female bee. This attracts the male bee to visit the flower and pollinate it.

Some plants use colors as a warning. The fly agaric toadstool is brightly colored to warn animals that it is poisonous.

Don't worry, it's visiting the colorful flowers.

Color in animals

When animals are colored to match their surroundings, we say they are camouflaged. It's difficult to spot a greeny-brown frog in a pond because the color of the pond matches the frog's skin. Animals use camouflage to hide from their enemies or stalk their prey.

The arctic fox has a white coat in winter, so it can hide in the snow. Its coat turns brown in summer, so it is camouflaged against the soil.

STANDING OUT

The poison arrow frog is bright red. This warns its enemies to keep away. Pick out some clothes which you think make you look striking.

I almost didn't see you in those colors!

You'd never believe it but...

Chameleons can change the color of their skin. They match their surroundings for camouflage and frighten enemies with the brightly colored insides of their mouths.

That's because I'm camouflaged.

Male peacocks (above left) have bright feathers to attract a mate. Female peacocks have dull feathers to camouflage them from enemies when they are sitting on their eggs.

Color messages

Colors can give us important information about what is happening all around us. The color red usually warns us of danger. A red traffic light means stop, and a green light means it's safe to go.

WAAAH!

MAKE A PAINT CHART
We say yellow is a warm color, perhaps because it reminds us of the sun. Cut out lots of colors. Place the colors you think are warm on one side of a piece of paper. Place the cold colors on the other side. Are there any colors you are not sure of?

How do you feel when you wake up and the sky is bright blue? Do you feel different when the sky is a dull gray? Colors can affect whether we feel happy or sad, relaxed or uncomfortable.

Help – you look really scary!

You'd never believe it but...

Colors for advertisements can be used to make us feel happy, sad, excited, or calm.

We sometimes use colors to describe how we feel. Have you ever felt "sad and blue," or "green with envy?" Can you think of any other expressions that use colors to describe your emotions?

Glossary

Absorb

To absorb means to take in. A sponge absorbs water. When light shines on an object, some of the colors in light are absorbed, and we don't see them. If all the colors are absorbed, we see black.

Camouflage

Some animals use camouflage to hide from their enemies. The colors of their coats or feathers are the same as their surroundings, so they are very difficult to see. Some animals use camouflage to hide when they stalk their prey.

Cones

Cones are a special kind of cell in your eyes that are sensitive to light. You have three kinds of cones — one kind that detects red light, another that detects blue light, and the third that detects green light.

Dye

We use dyes to color paints, materials, and many things we use. The color to make dyes can come from natural things, such as rocks or plants, or it can be made with chemicals.

Filter

Filters are made from transparent or see-through materials, like glass or cellophane, that have been colored. A filter only lets light of the same color pass through it, and it holds back the other colors. A green filter will only let through green light. A red filter will only let through red light.

Pigments

Pigments are natural colors found in soil, rocks, minerals, and plants. They can be used to make dyes that color the things we use.

Primary and secondary colors

The primary colors are red, blue, and yellow. The secondary colors are the colors you make when you mix any two of the primary colors together. Red and yellow make orange. Blue and yellow make green. Red and blue make purple. Orange, green, and purple are the secondary colors.

Prism

A prism is a piece of glass with triangle-shaped sides. When white light shines through a prism, it bends and splits into the seven colors of the spectrum.

Rainbow

A rainbow is a spectrum in the sky. It is the arc we see in the sky when sunlight shines through raindrops. The raindrops bend the white light and split it into the seven colors of the rainbow.

Reflect

To reflect means to send back or bounce back. When light shines on an object, we see the colors in light that bounce back off that object. If all the colors in light bounce back, we see white.

Spectrum

White light can be split into the seven colors of the rainbow. We call these colors the spectrum.

Transparent

Some materials, like glass or cellophane, are transparent. This means that they let light through and we can see through them.

Index

A
absorb 18, 20, 30

B
black 20, 21, 30

C
camouflage 26, 27, 30
chlorophyll 24
cones 19, 30

D
dyes 14, 15, 30

E
eyes 19, 30

F
filters 22, 23, 30
flowers 6, 13, 24, 25

I
inks 12, 13, 14
insects 6, 24, 25

L
light 5, 16, 18, 19, 20, 22, 23, 30, 31

O
opposites 10

P
paints 8, 9, 10, 11, 14, 28, 30, 31
pictures 9, 11
pigments 9, 14, 24, 31
plants 24, 25, 30, 31
primary colors 5, 8, 9, 10, 12, 31
prisms 21, 31

R
rainbows 5, 16, 17, 18, 20, 31
reflect 18, 20, 21, 31

S
secondary colors 5, 8, 31
shades 7, 9
spectrum 16, 20, 21, 31

T
transparent 22, 30, 31

W
white 16, 20, 21, 26, 30, 31

PHOTO CREDITS

Abbreviations: t-top, m-middle, b-bottom, r-right, l-left, c-center
All the photography in this book is by Roger Vlitos except the following pages: 9 — Frank Spooner Pictures; 11 — The National Gallery; 15 & 28 — Pictor International; 17, 26, 27 both — Bruce Coleman Collection; 19b & 25 — Spectrum Color Library; 20-21 — Simon Roose; 23t — Oxford Scientific Library.